Welcome Kindergarten!

written by
Sarah Jane Brian and María Angélica García

Reycraft Schoolhouse
145 Huguenot Street
New Rochelle, NY 10801

reycraftbooks.com

Reycraft Schoolhouse is a line of Reycraft Books, a trade imprint and trademark of Newmark Learning LLC.

Library of Congress Cataloging-in-Publication Data is available.

ISBN: 978-1-4788-9151-2 (A)

Photo Credits: Page 16A: Bob Ebbesen/Alamy; Page 19: Robert Kneschke/Alamy; Page 20B: Tetra Images/Alamy; Page 21C: Jim West/Alamy; Page 21D: Edwin Remsberg/Alamy; All other images from Shutterstock and Getty Images
Author photos: Billy Ray

Printed in Dongguan, China. 949559/1225/23628
10 9 8 7 6 5 4 3 2

First Edition published by Reycraft Schoolhouse 2025.

Reycraft Books and Newmark Learning LLC support diversity and the First Amendment, and celebrate the right to read.

To Yvonne Smith and Marilyn Martinez, my children's brilliant Kindergarten teachers. –S.J.B.

To my beloved son, Asdrúbal, who has taught me the importance of perseverance. –M.A.G.

Welcome to Kindergarten! Here we go.
Let's explore. There's so much to know!

How do students get to school? If you're like us . . .

You might arrive on a yellow school bus!

Some kids live nearby, and some travel far.
They walk to school or ride in a car.

The children all arrive at school, one by one and two by two.

Soon, it's time to go inside. Hello! Good morning! How are you?

The teacher waves and says, "Come on in!"
Now the day can really begin.

With a smile, a joke, and a high five too,
Teachers know just how to welcome you.

Clap!

In Kindergarten, we laugh and play,
Learning new things every day!

At first, the cubbies may all look the same,

Until the teacher helps you find your name.

Hang up your backpack
and look all around.

You'll see chairs that are just
the right size to sit down.

Go to a table, find your
name again,

And take a seat next to a
new friend.

On our classroom
rug we all can fit,

As we gather to listen
and speak while we sit.

Sometimes we work in groups of two or three.

Come read and play and learn with me!

Outside of our classroom are many more places,
And people to meet with friendly faces!

In the main office are different school staff,

Who help with our problems and even make us laugh.

The principal is in
charge of the school,

So we learn, stay safe,
and follow the rules.

In the library, you will find book after book.

Come on inside, and take a long look!

The librarian says, “Tell me, what interests you?

A book about tigers? A story that’s true?”

To read about dinosaurs, subways, or cats,
The librarian can find you a book about that.

Let's go to the gym or the yard for some fun!
One, two, three—get ready to run!

The P.E. teacher will put us through our paces,
From soccer to dancing to relay races.

We'll move and stretch and kick the ball,
To get healthy and strong, one and all.

Unzip your lunch bag,
or grab a tray.

It's time for a sandwich,
or the pasta of the day.

The cafeteria workers
prepare a tasty lunch,

Like chicken, and
tacos, and grapes—
a whole bunch!

Oh no, a spill! But that's okay.

A school custodian is on the way.

They clean, change lightbulbs, and have every door key.

They keep the school tidy and safe for you and me.

Make sure to help out—
put your trash in the bin.

To take care of our school,
we all need to chip in.

We've all worked so hard in our classroom today.

Let's take a break now, and go out to play!

At recess, we climb, run, and zoom down the slide,

Taking turns and showing kindness to friends by our side.

Zoom!

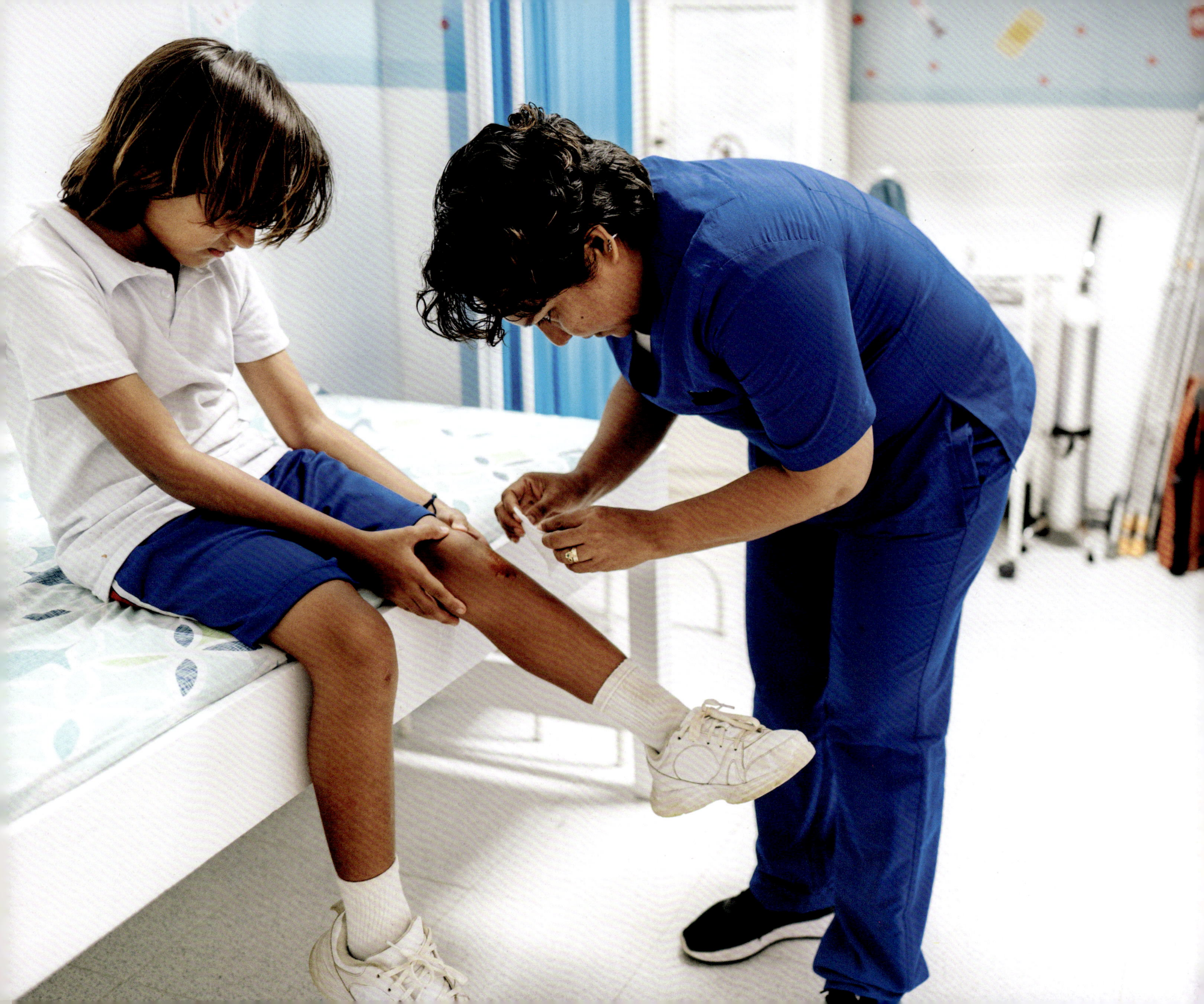

If you have a tummy ache or scrape your knee,
The school nurse's office is the place to be.

With a bandage and ice packs, the nurse cares for you.
If you need to lie down, there's a comfy cot, too.

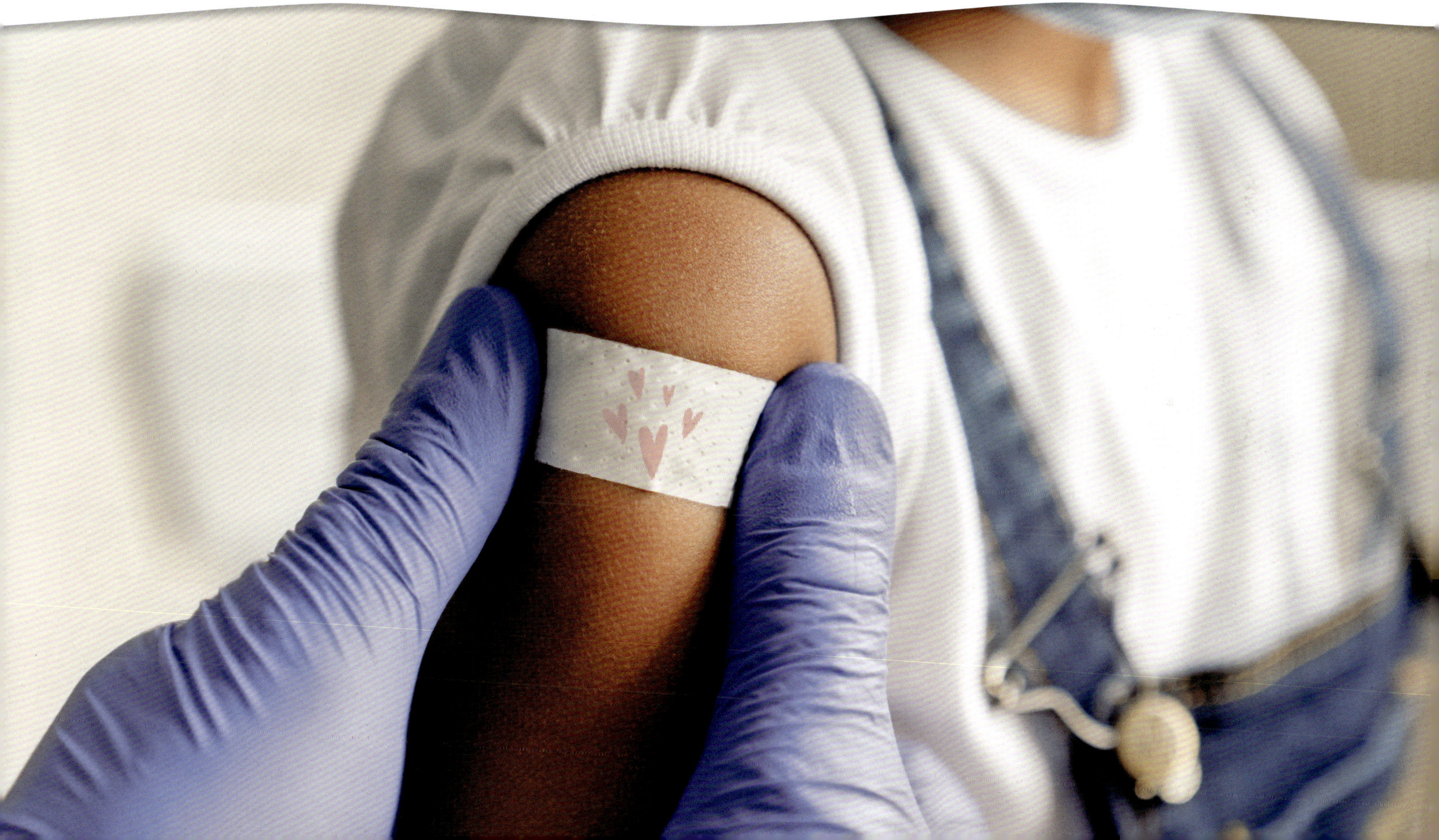

In music class, the teacher plays a song.
We dance and clap as we all sing along.

Clap,
clap,
clap!

Do you like to draw? It's time for art!
Let's make a monster or a heart.

I see crayons, paints, and paper to fetch.
We'll have so much fun as we paint, glue, and sketch.

We learned so much in Kindergarten today.
See you again tomorrow, hooray!

Grab your backpack, line up, and march to the door.
It's time to go home, but we'll be back for sure!

Bye!